The Hunt
FOR
GREEN
OCTOBERS

*A Practical Guide for the Job Seeker
and the Committed Careerist*

by

BOB RULE

Published by Luminary Media Group, an imprint of Pine Orchard, Inc.
Visit us on the internet at www.pineorchard.com

Printed in Canada.

9 8 7 6 5 4 3 2 1

ISBN 1-930580-33-9

Library of Congress Control Number: 2002100753

Cover photo of author, courtesy of *Alexander's / Houston, TX*

DEDICATION

— To Jan —
my wonderful wife
and mother of our three terrific sons
Rob, Roger, and Scott.

*Just like in staffing,
it's not who you are,
but who you have beside you.*

TABLE OF CONTENTS

FOREWORD

A recent survey of the top Human Resources executives of 100 major corporations revealed some unbelievable behaviors by people in the job search process:

- One candidate interrupted the interview to phone her therapist—seeking advice to answer a specific question.

- Another person said he was so well qualified that if he didn't get the job, it would prove that the company's management was incompetent.

- During one interview, an alarm clock went off in the candidate's briefcase. He took it out, shut it off, apologized for the interruption, and said he had to leave for another interview.

- And finally, how about the job seeker who asked the interviewer to put on a suit jacket to ensure that the offer was formal?

After reading some of these stories, it dawned on me that people might really need some additional help in reshaping their careers.

Albert Szent Gyorgyi once said: *"Research is to see what everybody else has seen, but to think what nobody else has thought."*

The same can be said about the job search process. Individually, the techniques described in the following pages are not revolutionary. However, when the described action plan is implemented in a structured approach, the results are often beneficial in re-starting one's career.

My profession as an executive recruiter has provided some unique insights in human behavior. Alas, the widespread perception of a headhunter's role is often misguided. It has always bothered me that people, no matter how savvy as a careerist, leave my office with the expectation that I will be their answer in satisfying their job search needs. They might as well expect their local grocery store owner to solve the problem of world hunger.

Most of the contents of this book were the outgrowth of two significant experiences: (1) When I started my first business, I quickly understood what was of greatest importance in the allocation of my time. Since I had zero customers, it was critical to have my smiling face in front of as many people as possible. Nothing happens in business until the idea or product is sold. This guidebook might serve as a simple primer on salesmanship, and some of the basics discovered in that embryonic effort are readily applied in self-marketing as a careerist. (2) After the initial location was established, I ventured to open a second office in Denver, Colorado. This launch was facilitated when I hired someone who possessed significant exposure in the outplacement business. Through his experiences, I began to realize how actions needed by job seekers were very different from the purposes of executive recruiters.

The ideas and processes outlined in *The Hunt for Green Octobers* have been shared with many people engaged in job search and/or career change. Like any other teaching, some concepts may be readily adopted by one, while others will select a different part of the menu. Rarely, however, has anyone executed *every* step of the process—probably due to the fact that the total program represents *a lot of work*.

You cannot imagine my pride when one of my sons, in need of coaching during a career transition, effectively implemented the playbook better than anyone in my past. And who says, *"A prophet is never appreciated in his own country"*?

And finally, it is my goal that levity and enjoyment can be found in the task of job searching or career redirection. It is so unfortunate that we often define ourselves by our professions. Most people spend more time at their jobs than with their spouse or children, so the importance of the results of the Hunt cannot be understated.

It takes more muscular effort to frown than to smile; it's a lot easier to grin than to cry. Such is true in your career. People who really want a job will eventually gain employment; but those who learn that the joy is in the journey and not the destination will experience the fruits a little earlier.

ABOUT THE AUTHOR

Bob Rule founded *BobRuleEnterprises* upon the completion of a 30-year career in human resource management, in both the corporate sector and the recruiting/staffing industry.

Previously, he founded Baker Street Group in 1990, a staffing services firm recognized twice by the *Houston 100* as one of the city's fastest growing companies. Baker Street Group acquired five different staffing firms; in 1997, BSG merged with StaffMark, a NASDAQ traded company with offices throughout the United States. Bob assumed an executive role directing all StaffMark commercial offices in the Western U.S. with operations that achieved revenues of over $125 million annually. In 1999, he was elected President of the Texas Association of Staffing.

He also founded W. Robert Michaels & Company in 1980, a retained executive search firm specializing in recruitment for oil and gas companies, financial service firms, and engineering/construction contractors. The Firm was successfully sold in 1987 and remains an on-going business entity. Subsequently, Mr. Rule served as Sr. Vice President-SW Region for a national temporary placement company, where he directed sales/service activities exceeding $30 million annually.

Bob's early professional development (1969-1979) occurred at Transco Energy Company and Tenneco, Inc. He advanced in key management roles in employment, compensation, affirmative action, and employee counseling. Mr. Rule earned his undergraduate degree in Business Administration from Rice University in 1969.

PART I

THE HUNT

GREEN OCTOBERS

October is one of my very favorite months. Any month that ushers in the World Series can't be all bad. If you live in Texas, October is the answering service for cooler weather—a welcome relief from the dog days of summer.

The tenth month of our calendar also signals a beginning for the titans of business—it is the starter's pistol that initiates the all important Fourth Quarter—and dictates whether it is winning time or whining time. It is the time when corporate America postures to deliver positive numbers to the Stock Market gods, or it is the time when management is otherwise forced to explain to its shareholders why next year will be better.

The singular negative to our Month of Hallows is the foliage that begins to shed from the trees. If only we could experience eternally Green Octobers. The non-stop raking and bagging of debris prevent me from spending an otherwise glorious Saturday afternoon on the golf course or viewing a great college football game. I also have to deal with the residue that is ceremoniously left behind by squirrels and other hibernating wild life. All the trash that they don't store in Santa's pouch for the upcoming freeze only complicates my yard work.

Green is the color of money. The accounting departments of corporate America are working furiously in October to find all the hidden operating results to guarantee smiles from the Boys of Wall Street and, eventually, the shareholders. Furthermore, green leaves <u>do not</u> reside in trash bags and <u>do not</u> prevent me from my tee time or tailgating pleasures.

 . . . The tenth month . . . dictates whether it is winning time or whining time.

The most successful careerists are *continually* engaged in the Hunt for Green Octobers because change in employment will occur several times in their career. Like the squirrels, we try to shape our careers so surplus acorns will be left in treasure chests to provide financial comforts during the changing seasons of our life. Unfortunately, too many careerists engage in the Hunt only when they are out of work and *need* a job, or when they get bored with their employer and *want* something new. When our needs and wants dictate our career choices, we are often left with limited options.

. . . Time . . . to deliver positive numbers . . . or it is the time when management is otherwise forced to explain to its shareholders why next year will be better.

In orchestrating a successful job search campaign, the careerist must address two basic questions:

- What is it that I want to do? **AND**
- How do I get there?

This book will only deal with the second question.

Obviously, the answer of the first question must come from within you, the reader. But even if you haven't clearly answered the question, the activity prescribed in the following chapters—those actions that dictate *how do I get there*—will often provide an insight of where you should be pointing in the first place.

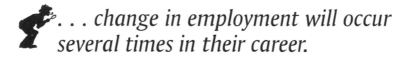 *. . . change in employment will occur several times in their career.*

In an ideal world, we would know the proper highway before the car was started to begin the journey. But I'm continually reminded of the wisdom of my dad: *"Do something, even if it's wrong!"* Nothing is more deadly to the job seeker than the inertia of waiting/analyzing/planning—invariably tweaking a resumé or waiting for lightning to strike from an internet job search engine. By the mere initiation of the journey, feedback will begin, and the successful careerist will digest the information, re-boot, and plot the actions and strategy necessary to answer both questions.

A colleague once said to me:

> *"Jobs don't exist; they emerge. No one is sitting at a desk with a requisition in his or her file cabinet with the name Bob Rule written at the top."*

A career evolves, not so much by luck, but by opportunity meeting preparedness. We must first plant seeds for the opportunity to spring forward, and then continually water the ground to ensure the preparedness.

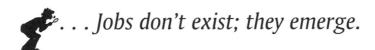 *. . . Jobs don't exist; they emerge.*

Too many careerists prefer to let someone else dictate their future opportunities. It amazes most people to learn that headhunters affect less than 8% of all job placements in the United States. It is erroneously assumed that executive search professionals are in the business of helping people find jobs. Rather, the essence of their profession is *helping clients find people.* Most professional headhunters do not proactively market candidates.

Approximately 9% of all job placements result from persons responding to a newspaper Help Wanted notice or Internet posting. Therefore, more than 80% of all jobs are still gained by one exercising his/her contacts. The old adage of "*not what you know, but who you know*" would seem to be in order. This simple handbook will <u>re-state</u> the adage to **"it's not only who knows you, but how well you manage them"** that ensures the successful Hunt for a continually Green October.

. . . It is erroneously assumed that executive search professionals are in the business of helping people find jobs. Rather, the essence of their profession is helping clients find people.

The role of staffing firms and other third parties participating in the marketplace will be examined. However, since headhunters, newspaper ads, and internet postings affect such a small percentage of the available jobs, this book focuses on a self-marketing plan—simple activities requiring only execution, delivered with a certain amount of finesse. The steps are not terribly difficult. They merely require the constitution and discipline of implementation.

The emotional challenges that face the person who loses his/her job is a pivotal issue, but it is only briefly discussed in a single chapter. Inner soul searching and self-analysis are required to overcome obstacles for the successful careerist; such introspection is the beginning of the *what is it that I want to do*" question. Additionally, this book only devotes one short chapter to resumé writing. There are entire books that will more completely address this topic.

Rather, I have placed the emphasis of this reading on executing basic sales techniques, repackaged in the form of a job search campaign, thus highlighting the most critical issue to achieving a Green October.

. . . a self-marketing plan—simple activities requiring only execution, delivered with a certain amount of finesse.

THE STAFFING INDUSTRY

It would be so much easier for a job seeker or committed careerist to simply contact a friend who is a search consultant ("headhunter"), and sit back and wait for the offers to roll in. The staffing industry, like many others, is very segmented and specific—with each component providing a different function. While it is important to include staffing professionals in your network, it must be remembered: *headhunters affect less than 8% of all job placements in the United States.* Much like a residential real estate agent, the *only* client is the payer of the fee—i.e., the seller of the home or the hiring company.

Each different niche in the staffing industry plays a different role. The term "executive search" is widely used (probably coined when the stuff-shirts in my business didn't like "headhunter"!) but it is not very descriptive. There are *retained* search consultants and *contingency-fee* search consultants.

The manner in which the search consultant is paid affects the way he/she works. Those working on a retainer (where a fee is paid to the search consultant by the hiring company whether or not the search is successful) are not as hurried in their work—i.e., their focus is to conduct the necessary research, interview every candidate personally, and prepare in-depth written reference and evaluation reports for the client. It is a slower and more thorough process—the consultant is not trying to beat the competition to get the first resumé to the client. The retainer ensures an exclusive engagement.

Contingent-fee search consultants, however, often accept the assignment with the knowledge that the same job order has been "listed" with another competitor. While many of these professionals are very thorough in their work, nonetheless, the pressure to submit resumés quickly does exist for obvious reasons. Furthermore, since the client has made no up-front commitment in the process, a job order is often placed with multiple firms, and later the company may decide not to fill the position or decide to promote someone internally.

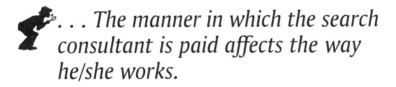 *. . . The manner in which the search consultant is paid affects the way he/she works.*

This does not happen as often in retained search because the client has invested time and money in the process. The contingent-fee search consultant may receive 50-75 "job orders" in a year and only fill 15-18 annually. A typical retained search consultant may be engaged only 12-15 times per year by a client, but should consummate nearly 100% of them in order to justify repeat business for future years. Retained search is more like a rifle shot; contingent search is slightly more shot-gunned. The exposure to multiple jobs is greater in the contingent world, but the contingent practitioner encounters far greater odds in consummation.

Neither type search consultant (retained or contingent) is actively marketing your candidacy to multiple prospective employers. There are, however, *placement firms* that work the "candidate side of the street." Such firms (also working on a contingent fee paid by the hiring company) are not nearly as prevalent as their "executive search" counterparts, and they are *typically* engaged in somewhat lower level jobs. Placement firms will aggressively telemarket to numerous potential employers their "inventory" of candidates. The service to the candidate is not very personal, but a far greater exposure to the marketplace occurs for the candidate.

. . . Retained search is more like a rifle shot; contingent search is slightly more shot-gunned.

Many people engaged in the Hunt often mistake search/ placement consultants with **outplacement consultants.** Outplacement is a professional service much more akin to training—i.e., providing assistance in assessment of career path options, resumé writing, encouragement in *self-marketing,* interview coaching, and sometimes, office facilities. Like the search business, there are two different sectors of the outplacement world.

I have labeled the service provider that charges fees directly to the job seeker as being in the *retail* outplacement business. Similar services are often paid for by the employer when forced to terminate an employee, whether for non-performance or as a reduction-in-force. These firms, retained by companies in such situations, might be called *corporate* outplacement providers. Once again, both the retail and corporate outplacement firms do not find an individual a job, but rather, provide assistance in the job search process.

Temporary and/or contract staffing firms provide yet another niche. In such a relationship, the candidate interviews with the staffing firm who attempts to affect placement with a client company. If there is a resulting match, the candidate is legally an employee of the staffing firm, not the company that provides the work assignment. Temporary/contract staffing firms exist at every level of the employment marketplace—light industrial, office and clerical, specialty medical (including doctors!), accountants, engineers, systems professionals, and even senior level executives. These firms provide a wonderful bridge to full-time employment, but it is in the best interest of this type of staffing firm for the candidate to remain as an employee on their payroll.

. . . Outplacement is a professional service much more akin to training— providing assistance in assessment of career path options, resumé writing, encouragement in self-marketing, and interview coaching . . . .

Other than this brief overview, our October Hunt will <u>not</u> focus on staffing firms, but rather *self-marketing processes.* Job seekers and committed careerists seeking <u>full-time</u> employment should be focusing most of their time on the 80% (plus) of the available opportunities, not the 8% represented by the staffing industry.

THE REFLECTION IN THE MIRROR

The attitude of the careerist entering the job search process often varies with the circumstances motivating the change. For the person who has been terminated from a job, the feelings of anger and guilt are generally pervasive. For the otherwise unemployed, a sense of uncertainty, coupled with some element of fear is normal. The careerist who is employed but seeking to make a change is often secretive—obviously wishing to shield the search campaign from the existing employer. All of these inner feelings serve as a hindrance (or at least are limiting factors) to an effective self-marketing campaign.

If you've never been fired, don't ever say to an affected person *"I know how you feel."* It is terrible. All of the trite comments like *"things happen for a reason"* or *"there is something better out there"* may well be true, but intensely destructive feelings often linger. The feelings are normal and natural—**but get over it.** Effectiveness in orchestrating a change in career cannot begin until the person affected looks in the mirror and likes what he/she sees. The occurrence of job termination has some similarity to the death of a loved one or to a divorce, and takes a period of time for the mourning process to run its course.

For the otherwise unemployed beginning the Hunt, apprehension and excitement are likely occurring simultaneously. There is not as much to overcome (guilt and anger are much more destructive); but, nonetheless, the aspect of CHANGE is often frightening. Change is a word that very few people embrace with zest. Conversely, the word CHALLENGE conjures positive images. In dealing with the inner struggle between dreaded *change* and exhilarating *challenge,* it should always be remembered that the only difference in these diverse words is just three little letters—L, L, and E *(change* and *cha*(**lle**)*nge).* Once again, the person who is reflected in the mirror must remove apprehension before the zest is truly effective.

. . . The occurrence of job termination has some similarity to the death of a loved one or to a divorce, and takes a period of time for the mourning process to run its course.

Understandably, an employed person will guard confidentiality; but the privacy sought is counterproductive to a *rapid search campaign.* In the ensuing chapters, the high activity required in a self-marketing campaign will be evident. The more the candidate "remains in the closet," the slower the pace of the job search. There is not an obvious solution to this dilemma; but the employed person must simply recognize that the time required for change is extended by the amount of confidentiality needed.

In the last 30 years of the 20th Century, attitudes regarding job change and unemployment began to change dramatically. Prior to that time, the goal of our parents and grandparents was to work for a single employer for a career, receive the gold watch, and retire happily ever after. As time progressed, it seemed permissible to occasionally change jobs, but only if there was another job already in place for the careerist to assume.

With the implosion of corporate America, business leaders begin to realize that if it was permissible for the <u>employee</u> to change the invisible employment contract, then it was also fair for the <u>employer</u> to effect reductions-in-force when needed. The result placed great talent in the marketplace, which served as a boom for entrepreneurs and small business. With this change, the mindset of "cradle to grave" employment evaporated, and thus, the social stigma of unemployment was minimized.

The speed of change is accelerating at unbelievable rates. There was a span of 112 years (1727-1839) between the origins of photography and the commercial reproduction of cameras. The comparable span of time with the telephone was shortened to 56 years (1820-1876); with television, just 12 years (1922-1934); and with the transistor, only 5 years (1948-1953). Today, miracle drugs are created in less than a year; technology changes so quickly that it represents learning challenges even for our kids! As our education becomes obsolete, it is likely that we will change *careers* numerous times, not to mention *job* changes.

. . . With the implosion of corporate America, business leaders begin to realize that if it was permissible for the employee to change the invisible employment contract, then it was also fair for the employer to effect reductions-in-force when needed.

It is the fear of failure or rejection that constipates us during changing times. It is amazing to reflect on our many failures that we no longer remember. We fell down the first time we tried to walk and almost drowned the first time we tried to swim. Our first word was unintelligible; learning to tie shoes required long practice. Lest we also forget that R.H. Macy failed seven times before his store in New York was successful. Babe Ruth struck out 1330 times, but also hit 714 home runs. Since one's best work often occurs when there is an element of pressure or a deadline to meet, then it makes sense that similar circumstances in a job search campaign might also prove helpful.

. . . It is the fear of failure or rejection that constipates us during changing times.

The manner in which we embrace change can take three very different forms: compliance, identification, or internalization.

Many people deal with change out of <u>compliance.</u> This is a childlike behavior. We act because we are told to: *"Sit up."* *"Eat your green beans."* *"Don't speak with your mouth full."* Behaviors resulting from this type of change management are often instant, but not long lasting.

Secondly, people encounter change by <u>identification</u>—a teenage behavior. We act in a manner that is expected of us; we do as the group dictates. In career decisions, we often act due to pressure imposed by peers, a spouse, friend, or neighbor.

In a perfect world, we change due to <u>internalization</u>—the adult manifestation of change management. When we have authorship of the idea and act because of our own internal feelings, the career result is long-lasting and rewarding. Sadly, this type of change often requires an extended time period to accomplish.

Most changes of job seekers and committed careerists are a result of balancing all three factors into a **blended** solution.

These drivers of change—compliance, identification, and internalization—may seem, on the surface, to be rather abstract, not in keeping with Green October's promise to be a *"Practical Guide."*

I was introduced to these thoughts many years ago when my church was preparing the congregation for an impending, dramatic change. The person leading the seminar spent hours teaching how individuals react to change under these three different influences. Finally, she put the concepts into focus when she said:

> *"These terms—compliance, identification, and internalization—have an even greater relevance when one considers the Christian understanding of the Trinity. God reflected Himself to mankind with these same three driving forces. In Old Testament times, the Law was issued, a form of compliance. But, when mankind continued to reject the Law, He decided to send a Messiah with whom man could identify. Rejection continued. But, when the Spirit was internalized, coupled with the laws of Compliance and the reality of the Identifier, change was personal and long lasting."*

Obviously, the careerist needs to comply with the laws of the marketplace as a framework for decision making. Change motivated by a peer group or loved ones is practical and healthy. But, when these factors are properly **blended** with one's own internal drivers, empowerment can truly begin.

... Most changes of job seekers and committed careerists are a result of balancing all three factors into a blended solution.

If emotions range from anger, guilt, uncertainty, or fear—if there is an abnormal need for confidentiality—if the thrill of challenge does not overcome the agony of change—then the self-marketing campaign is stymied. There are professionals, far more studied than I, who help people deal with issues of self-image. Many of the negative feelings are real and, depending on the circumstances, predictable. Often, time heals wounds; but time can also bury negative behaviors that may resurface at an inopportune moment in the future.

Since the self-marketing campaign that we are about to explore requires high energy and a propensity for action, the person looking into the mirror must first be cleansed of limiting factors before engaging in the Hunt.

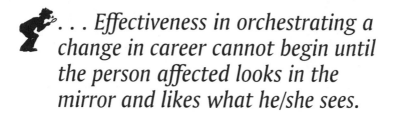 *. . . Effectiveness in orchestrating a change in career cannot begin until the person affected looks in the mirror and likes what he/she sees.*

PART II

THE
SELF-MARKETING
CAMPAIGN

A POLICY AND PROCEDURE WRITER?

The word "networking" really jumped into our consciousness in the late 80's. The computer geeks thought they discovered the Holy Grail when they figured out how to make one computer talk to another. However, successful sales professionals perfected networking long before Bill Gates became rich. They have long since known that cold calls seldom produce warm results, and have relied on contacts to open doors, establish relationships, and thus, zero in on the prospect. Salesmanship is merely networking perfected.

Very few careerists wish to consider themselves as a salesman. The art of "peddling" doesn't rank highly in the minds of the American public. Words like "polyester" and "snake oil" come to mind when thinking of salesmen. And, if you added the adjective *telephone* to salesman, the negative thoughts jump off the Richter scale. People engaged in the Hunt for Green Octobers quickly embrace the fact that they are selling a product very near and dear to their hearts: *Themselves.*

 . . . Salesmanship is merely networking perfected.

My first experience as a networker had its predictable ups and downs. In 1969, I was a freshly minted graduate from Rice University, only to find out that the employers were not lining up to put me on their payroll. I had reasonably academic successes, participated in intercollegiate sports, wore a new suit, and didn't smell. Maybe my approach to becoming a Management Trainee was wrong.

For approximately two months, I trudged the streets of Houston, Texas, filling out applications, smiling as sweetly as possible at all of the friendly receptionists. Predictably, I also received an impressive stack of "NO" letters—but all came with the assurance that the prospective employers "had taken the liberty of retaining my resumé in their *active* files." After another month of waiting, it became apparent that their files were not all that active.

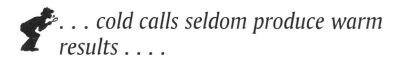 *. . . cold calls seldom produce warm results . . . .*

One day the telephone rang, not from a potential employer, but from my long-time source of income—Dad. After politely inquiring about my prospects (likely fearful that I would remain on his payroll), he finally suggested a call to one of his distant business acquaintances—the Corporate Secretary at Tenneco,

Inc. Like most all-knowing college graduates, I winced at the suggestion. It was obvious to me that the Corporate Secretary at Tenneco was just someone who took dictation. But, being the ever-dutiful son and because I had nothing else to do, I called the number provided by Dad and was granted the appointment.

Upon arrival at the 30th floor of the Tenneco building, which happened to be the top floor, it began to dawn on me that perhaps the Corporate Secretary had other people taking dictation for him. Entering an office with the square footage that approached the entire state of Rhode Island, I began to realize how much smarter my dad was becoming. To my disappointment, however, the interview was very brief. At the conclusion of a 250-second chat, he finally offered:

"You seem like a nice young man. Let me take you down to the Personnel Office." (The term "Human Resources" had not been invented then.)

The interview with the Personnel guy was also less than probing. As I patiently answered every question, my prayer was that he would not drop off to sleep while listening to my stimulating answers. But suddenly, for no apparent reason, he lurched forward, as if remembering that I *was* referred from the 30th floor, and blurted out:

"We do have one job that might be appropriate for a recent college graduate. How would you like to be a Policy and Procedure Writer?"

Blinking only slightly, I took a deep breath and responded that "such a challenge had been a career goal of mine." (The job paid $700/month; therefore, I could afford an apartment, be on the lookout for Houston's most eligible single women, and not live with Mom and Dad.)

The final step of the process was the most amazing, however. My new best friend, Personnel Genius, took me down to meet the hiring authority. My jaw dropped as we were introduced— the hiring authority was the father of a young lady that I dated in college, and amazingly, I got the job. *Why?*

I later learned that he had interviewed four other candidates, all with experiences in writing policies and procedures. I did not know that people actually did that kind of work, and yet I got the job. Furthermore, I had been none too gentle when I "dumped" his daughter for what seemed like a more promising prospect.

Why did I get the job?

Thirty years later, the answer seems clear. Upon "further review" (as NFL referees say), three truisms of career networking have crystallized in my mind.

1. Always start as high in the targeted organization as possible. Top people have a huge influence on mid-level decision makers. Personnel Genius would have never awakened in the interview without a "proper" introduction. Top people also know other top people. If you can get an audience with <u>any</u> influential person, even if such person has nothing to do with your targeted job function, the meeting is time well spent. Too many job seekers limit their focus to visiting with people in their chosen path of work. If you are a Policy and Procedure Writer but can obtain an audience with a well-known Neurosurgeon, do yourself a favor and proceed, posthaste. It is surprising the wonderful doors that can be opened by top level people.

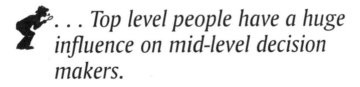 *. . . Top level people have a huge influence on mid-level decision makers.*

---

2. Careerists often "screen out" ideas not to their liking too early in the process. When you've worked hard to get an appointment, take the time to listen to ALL the ideas and suggestions offered by your networking mentor. An early cold shoulder to an idea can inhibit further ideas; *thus, embrace every suggestion as "your career goal."*

In no way does this suggest that you should accept any job offered in the Hunt. But, as conversation is progressing, always remember that the only offer to be rejected is the offer you *actually* receive. No considerations need to be made until a job offer is forthcoming. While networking, you are to seek the ideas of others. If your networked target thinks it is a good idea for you to follow along (and if you are networking with top level people), then it might be wise to play Follow the Leader.

3. At the end of the road, you will probably find that the person who finally pulls the trigger and offers the job of your choosing will likely be someone of your *distant* past. Most job seekers prefer to network with people that they know well because there is less rejection by "friends."

However, there is an axiom in employment: "Only Perfect Candidates Are Hired." Not surprisingly, the Company will later learn that the newly hired perfect candidate makes a mistake or two and joins the ranks of mere mortals a few weeks into the job. Your close friends know your skill sets well, but they also know your warts and blemishes. Fortunately for you, however, persons from your *distant* past may view your credentials as *perfect*.

I have often outlined the techniques of the job search process and frequently have asked the participant: *"How many people do you know that can help you find the right job?"* Sadly, the responses are consistent. Three, five, eight—are the typical answers. At that point, the participant received my admonishment for not profiting from my early experience.

> *"The guy who pulled the trigger and hired me was the father of a girl I dated in college. I dated a lot of different girls and they all had fathers, too!"*

The size of your network is almost infinite. The numbers are limited only by the number of people you have met in life. The joy of the successful careerist is to "funnel down" the network into a consistent, persistent plan of action. When I hear someone in a job search say, *"My network has dried up,"* I know that he/she has never really started.

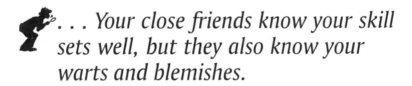 *. . . Your close friends know your skill sets well, but they also know your warts and blemishes.*

Networking requires an adjustment in the thinking of most careerists. One must wear the shoes of a sales professional comfortably, and perfect those skills during the Hunt. And, most importantly, one must realize that the most qualified person is seldom hired. Tenneco can attest to that fact.

The Self-Marketing Campaign
DEFINING THE NETWORK

So, how many people do you know that can help you find the *right* job? Targeting the suspect is not as difficult as one might think. The task begins with writing (and continually maintaining) a minimum listing of 250 people that can play a role in your Hunt. It is always fun to watch people gulp at the suggestion of 250 as the minimum target number. (Remember, the list includes everyone you have met in your life.)

When I started my headhunting career in 1980, my first task was to market my services. The initial source for 250 names came from my business calendars in 1977-1979. To my surprise, I met with 173 people "from the outside world," i.e., people not employed by the Company for whom I was working. My secretary also maintained a copy of all the "While You Were Out" messages—the dreaded pink slip that meant you had to return phone calls. I was delighted to find numerous new names of people that wanted to contact me. Now I was preparing to contact them!

. . . The task begins with writing (and continually maintaining) a minimum listing of 250 people that can play a role in your Hunt.

Alumni directories, membership rosters of professional associations, and even church and neighborhood phone books provide ample names to start a networking list. Previous vendors, relatives of friends and associates, and "the fathers of *all* the girls you dated in college" can greatly inflate this exercise, particularly if you were socially active! The most important part of the exercise is to "data dump" any name that comes to mind. Screen in; don't screen out. Search your mind for anyone who can at least recall your name. Even if you are a Policy and Procedure Writer, be sure to include all your acquaintances who are Rocket Scientists and Neurosurgeons. Any list worth compiling for such an important task is not to be rushed. Take several days, let the names simmer, research to add others, and let your mind wander to new heights.

The record keeping aspect of this new data will prove to become invaluable. Many years ago, I maintained a simple three-ring notebook with the name of all my contacts, filed in order of the Company name, noting addresses and telephone numbers.

However, the most important notations were the dates and summaries of every conversation that I made with that suspect.

Early in my career, I copied the style of a particularly adept sales professional who marketed services to me. He would start his conversations by saying:

> *"We last spoke on 'X' date and in that conversation, you indicated _____ ."*

In this manner, I was "on notice" that I was being "tracked," thus adding importance to the conversation. Fortunately today, numerous computerized contact information systems will store and retrieve that information in a far more effective way. The careerist must merely enter and update the information.

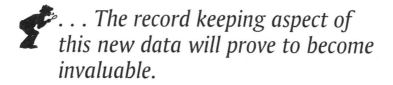 *. . . The record keeping aspect of this new data will prove to become invaluable.*

The more difficult task of shaping the network for your career purposes is to eliminate 225 of the 250 names that you worked so hard to compile. It is almost impossible to process more than 25 contacts at one time. (Immediately, I can read your mind: *If I'm only going to work with 25 people in my network, I'll just write down 25 names!)* The only way to ensure the list is a product of <u>good</u> habits rather than <u>bad</u> habits is to exercise the discipline of emptying your mind and uncovering your past. When you look back to view the *best* 25 names, my guess is that you will find the real diamonds didn't surface until your roster exceeded the initial 100-150 of the anticipated suspects.

Who are the *best* 25? If you have embraced the premise in the previous chapter, the best 25 would be the highest level people on the list (regardless of their alignment to your career path)— and those persons from your distant past.

The mental breakthrough occurs when the successful careerist realizes that he/she has encountered more people than first imaginable. Our good friends—or even people that we see often—come to mind easily. To assume that some highly influential person won't remember you is Step One in defeat. It may require a gentle reminder to place your meeting or relationship into the setting of your acquaintanceship, but the rewards far outweigh the occasional embarrassment of rejection.

" . . . We last spoke on 'X' date and in that conversation, you indicated _____."

Top level, influential people often soar to great heights because they, too, have maintained an awareness of people they have met or observed in their past. In 1984, it was an honor to be introduced to the former Governor of Texas, the Honorable Mark White. My host was taking great pains explaining my background to "justify" our meeting. However, White cut short my long-winded friend by merely saying:

> *"I know who Bob is—he made two free throws against my Baylor Bears that beat us in the last few seconds of a game."*

I was amazed. As a second-string basketball player who, 15 years previously, had one lucky opportunity to be a hero, it was shocking that he recalled my name. Our previous "introduction" occurred when he was a *spectator* at a rather insignificant basketball game.

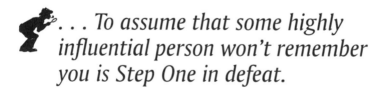 *. . . To assume that some highly influential person won't remember you is Step One in defeat.*

High level people often have a high level memory—or they will bluff it, even if their recall has temporarily faded. Successful careerists call to memory the top level people that they have met or know—and then depend on their executive egos or amazing abilities to remember you.

...Targeting the suspect is not as difficult as one might think. . . . the mental breakthrough occurs when the successful careerist realizes that he/she has encountered more people than first imaginable.

The Self-Marketing Campaign
CONTACTING THE SUSPECTS

Telemarketers are engaged in perhaps one of the least loved professions in our society. Few people aspire to becoming the caller who interrupts the dinner hour of the general public to pitch the latest and greatest offering of corporate America. Furthermore, the training for this difficult work is slipshod, at best. This having been said, it makes perfect sense that the successful careerist, who is now clearly defined as a salesman, will take every precaution to minimize the time spent (and the information dispensed) over the phone.

This is not to say that telephone usage can be avoided in the process. It is still the primary communications tool utilized by most business professionals. But the object in successful networking is to get "face time" with the intended audience. However, all too many job seekers mistakenly communicate an excessive amount of information in the initial contact call, thus, providing opportunities to "screen out" the desired appointment.

 . . . the object in successful networking is to get "face time" with the intended audience.

After the listing of "the *best* 25" has been properly formulated, it is time to march forward and secure the appointment. Regardless of how well you know the person, it is *always* best to write a letter that you will be calling to ask for a personal meeting. In this manner, the telemarketing time is minimized. It is much easier to control a message in planned written communication than to engage in a free-flowing phone conversation that can take off in any direction.

However, the eventual success of this letter is often dependent upon the amount of homework completed prior to it being sent. The first step is to call the company switchboard to verify the spelling of each name being written, the *exact* manner in which the company name is presented, the correct mailing address, and a direct dial number, if possible. This process is recommended even if you possess a business card of your intended target. Cards become outdated in rapid order considering the constant reorganization of corporate America. The call will also provide an opportunity to seek directions to the office that you hope to visit.

A second call can then be made to speak to the Executive Assistant of the person that you will be writing. In this call, you will be able to confirm the information that has already been provided. (Who knows the competency of the person at the switchboard?) But the most critical point of this step is to interject into the conversation with saying, *"By the way, may I have your name, please?"*

Sally Sue is a VIP in this process and it is important to establish a first name familiarity. It is appropriate to conclude the dialogue by saying:

> *"I'll be sending Fred* (your target) *some correspondence in the next day or so, and I just wanted to have the correct contact information."*

With this comment, Sally Sue is on the lookout for your letter, and hopefully your intonation left a positive feeling.

Armed with the appropriate information, it is time to write the letter—but not before a visit to the stationery shop to select the appropriate medium. Its appearance must be tailored to convey the intended message. Generally speaking, white, beige, or light gray tones send the most professional message. The weight and texture of the paper add to the message. Special touches, such as embossing, add class but increase the expense.

Considering the capabilities of high quality (not dot matrix) computer printers to create a personal letterhead, other creative notations might be overkill. Persons seeking a career path in more artistic professions would naturally consider a more dramatic presentation than the normal corporate America look. Coordination with matching envelopes is essential to complete the finished product.

The recommended transmittal letter crafted to accompany the resumé about to be sent should be five sentences, three paragraphs, and would read something like this:

Dear Joe, **(First name presumes familiarity; you are hoping to get familiar, quickly!)**

We sat at the same table with Bill Jones at last year's Southwest Human Resources Annual Conference. **(i.e., this is how I know you; if Joe was referred to you by someone else, this is the place to be a name dropper!)**

Enclosed is my biographical summary reflecting 23 years experience in human resources management, in both the corporate sector and the recruiting/staffing industry. **(i.e., enclosed is my resumé.)** Of particular note, I am skilled in organizational development processes dealing with human capital integration that is necessary in business mergers and acquisitions. **(i.e., here is a singular aspect of my multiple skill sets that I want to highlight.)** This aspect of my career has produced my best work and greatest professional joys.

I will call you in the next few days to request a time when we might visit. **(Make note: this sentence does NOT say, "If you have interest for someone of my skills, please call me.")**

Warm regards,

Alfred T. Applicant

Alfred T. Applicant

Several points are worth considering in reviewing the letter from Alfred T. Applicant:

1. First, it is short and to the point. Few business people carefully read transmittal letters, and it must grab their attention quickly.

2. The first and last paragraphs are each one sentence. These are the two most important sentences in the letter. Only the first sentence needs to be changed in every case, thus the letter is easily mass-produced.

3. Depending upon the recipient of the letter, it might be advantageous to alter the second sentence of the second paragraph (i.e., stress differing skill sets to differing readers).

4. When the letters are finally mailed to the *best* 25 targets, be mindful that all 25 will require a follow-up phone call. Therefore, it would probably be wise to mail the first 8 letters on Monday, the next 8 on Wednesday, and the remainder on Friday. Thus, the follow-up call can be spaced in a comfortable manner.

It seems so much easier to just pick up the phone to "reach out and touch someone" to accelerate the process of securing an appointment. Written communication, however, is especially effective to impart messages of great importance. And to a successful careerist, any appointment is of great importance.

By writing in advance, the message is controlled and planned, and the recipient receives the information at a time of his/her convenience, rather than field a call in the hurry of the day. But the greatest benefit of writing in advance is that the careerist minimizes telemarketing—a job that is difficult at best, not appreciated, and for which very few people are well trained.

. . . Written communication . . . is especially effective to impart messages of great importance. . . . By writing in advance, the message is controlled and planned . . .

All successful sales professionals can't wait to exit the office and "get out into the field." The idea of completing research tasks and then writing letters or doing reports is the very bane of their existence. Since the *successful* careerist is first and foremost in the sales business, it should come as a welcome relief to be in the action mode of arranging and securing "face time."

Now is the time to engage Ma Bell in the process; it is time to dial for dollars. Considerable effort has been expended in securing the appropriate contact information, and typically the first person to whom we speak is our old friend Sally Sue, the Executive Assistant of Public Suspect #1 (who from this point forward will be Friendly Fred).

> ALFRED: Hi, Sally Sue, this is Alfred T. Applicant. Is Fred available?
>
> SALLY SUE: I'm sorry, Alfred, he's not available right now. May I take a message or put you through to his voice mail?

The natural tendency is to comply and leave a message. We have become almost numb to playing "telephone tag" in the normal course of business operations, so why not repeat the behavior as a careerist?

But consider this point. If you were trying to become the scoring champion of the National Basketball Association, would you want to shoot the ball or pass it? To my best recollection, it is hard to score when someone else has the ball, so therefore, I would not be anxious to relinquish control—at least, not at this early stage of the communication. Thus, the appropriate response is:

```
   ALFRED: Gee, Sally Sue—I'm in a workshop
           outside of the office, and I was just
           calling during a break. Fred will
           have difficulty in reaching me with a
           return call today. Is there a time
           when I might be able to step out and
           call him back?

SALLY SUE: He should be free this afternoon—I
           don't see anything on his calendar
           after 3:00 pm.

   ALFRED: That will be perfect. We should have
           another break about that time, and
           I'll call him back then. Thanks, and
           have a great day!
```

Throughout the job search process, it is imperative to maintain control at all possible stages. Whenever your message is sent to voice mail, you have lost control. The call may (or may not) be returned; or if it is returned, you may be unavailable. Don't pass the ball now. Allowing the call to be sent to voice mail might make you the assist leader in the NBA, but not the scoring champion. You've got another chance at 3:00 pm.

ALFRED: Hi, Sally Sue, this is Alfred T. again. Is Fred available now?

SALLY SUE: I'm sorry, Alfred, I thought he would be free—but an unexpected meeting just came up. I know he'll be free in about 15 minutes. I'll be happy to take your number and have him call you back.

ALFRED: Well, unfortunately, Sally Sue, the workshop is about ready to start again and I'll be unreachable. Will he be in tomorrow?

SALLY SUE: Yes, sir, he should be in all day.

ALFRED: Thanks a lot, Sally Sue. Just tell him to expect my call then. Have a great evening!

The unsuspecting Sally Sue probably assumes that your onslaught for the day is over—but surprise! If, during your research to write the transmittal letter to accompany your resumé, you secured a direct dial number for Fred, then a third call can be made that day—at about 5:45 pm—when Sally Sue has left, but perhaps, not Fred. There is yet another opportunity to reach Fred (without talking to Sally Sue)—and that is at 7:25 am the next day. It is not uncommon for Fred to work later in the day or earlier in the morning than his Executive Assistant.

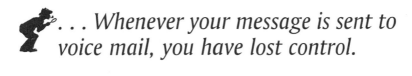 *. . . Whenever your message is sent to voice mail, you have lost control.*

An Executive Assistant often provides a screen to your target. Thus, Fred remains in control, not you. As you can see, we are at counter purposes here! We are not trying to manage around Sally Sue because she is a bad person, but she does interrupt your quest for a scoring title. Your goal is simply to *initiate* contact with Fred (so that you are fully prepared), rather than to respond to his return call (if it is forthcoming). Obviously, at some point in the process, Sally Sue might become unavoidable. You can only be "out of pocket" for so long. Some calls will have to be returned, but certainly not before every effort is expended to be the initiator.

At long last, Gabriel's trumpet has sounded, and we are finally able to speak to Fred. Since we don't get a second chance to make a first impression, the critical moment has arrived. The natural tendency is to strive for a warm and lengthy dialogue—one which starts with entertaining chit chat, embraces heartfelt family and social needs, and then gently eases into the brilliance of your sterling qualifications as the world's premier Policy and Procedure Writer. **WRONG.**

. . . Your goal is simply to initiate contact with Fred . . . rather than respond to his return call . . . .

The central purpose of mailing the transmittal letter and resumé in advance was to minimize your time on the telephone. Fred has been alerted of the nature of your call by carefully crafted correspondence, and you have invested in the Pony Express for delivery. Once again, it is time to be short and to the point— and not detract from anything that you might wish to say when you have "face time."

> ALFRED: Hi, Fred, this is Alfred T.
> Applicant. A few days ago I forwarded some correspondence alerting you of my call. I would appreciate 20-30 minutes of your time. Do you have an opening next Tuesday or does Thursday work better for your schedule?

The technique of ending with this question is known as the *presumed close.* You are framing your question with the assumption that Fred wants to see you; the only uncertainty is when. Furthermore, the implication is that Fred doesn't need to ask many questions, because a transmittal letter and resumé have already been forwarded. *Just answer Yes or No, Fred!*

. . . The central purpose of mailing the transmittal letter and resumé in advance was to minimize your time on the telephone.

The moment of truth has arrived and all salespeople hold their collective breath waiting for the response. If the answer is Yes, then book the time and get off the phone. All dialogue is better said face-to-face.

What about another answer? The most common one is:

> FRED: Alfred, I did receive your resumé—and you certainly have a strong background. Unfortunately, we are just not hiring right now, and I wouldn't want to waste your time.

The fork in the road has finally presented itself. Which way do we go? Play nice guy and hang up with our tail between our legs—or do we "overcome the objection"? I'll leave it to your imagination as to what *successful* sales professionals do. The trick is to shift the context of Fred's response so that we are not challenging his decision, but rather re-formatting the question being asked. This requires the theater skills of all good thespians.

> ALFRED: Oh Fred, I'm sorry—my letter was probably not clear. I didn't write you with the supposition that General Motors **(Fred's company)** is hiring. I know that Bill Jones **(reference the first sentence of the transmittal letter)** thinks a lot of you, and he felt that you could be of some assistance to me. I've got an idea or two and I'd like to pick your brain and get your input. A phone call won't do this justice, but I'll limit the time required to less than 20 minutes. What's good for your schedule?

More flies are caught with honey than vinegar. If Fred has tried the screen-out approach, the best way to accomplish your purposes (overcome the objection) is to re-position the scenario and then flatter Fred without the appearance of manipulation. But it is worth noting, your conversation always closes with asking for an appointment time. (Ask for the order!)

. . . The trick is to shift the context of Fred's response so that we are not challenging his decision, but rather re-formatting the question being asked.

We have redefined the request for an *informational* interview rather than a job interview. All you want is the opportunity to see Fred so that you can extend the sales process. Seldom is a sale consummated on the first call, but a sale is never consummated unless the first appointment is granted.

No technique works 100% of the time. Not surprisingly, even the best networker hears "NO"—or in cases where Fred was a total jerk, phone calls don't get returned. The successful careerist develops a thick skin, recognizes that rejection is a part of the sales process, and moves on while never regarding the "NO" as a defeat.

I always maintained statistics to measure what percentage of the "suspects" were successfully converted into an appointment. Time and energy has been spent to correspond with the *best* 25, but realistically, the goal was to secure 15-18 appointments. If a 60%-70% success ratio is not achieved, then it becomes a simple matter to send out a few more letters. Take delight, however, in achieving the successful percentage (of YES) that you have set for yourself.

The NO's have temporarily lost an opportunity to meet you, but they should still receive a handwritten thank you note for spending time with you on the phone (or just reviewing your resumé). At a later date, you might elect to have someone call on your behalf.

The seas have parted, and the sky has cleared. Fred said, "Yes." All is well with Gabriel and the rest of the world. Showtime has just begun. Several thoughts should be considered in preparation for the appointment.

1. Alfred T. has invested considerable energies to *obtain* the appointment, but now needs to dedicate a similar time commitment to ensure its success. Most companies have web sites that provide a wealth of information to educate Alfred on the nature of Fred's business and perhaps recent events that have merited press releases. Often, names of other management personnel are listed and ideally, Alfred will be able to establish a connection to someone else in the company who knows Fred. A review of the annual report prior to meeting Fred provides additional information.

2. Psychologists generally agree that most interview decisions are made in the first 4-5 minutes of the initial visit. Much of the decision making is guided by appearances and non-verbal communications. Therefore, the actual words that you do say in the first 4-5 minutes are critical. Most of these meetings start with an introductory chit-chat—so these are the words to be most carefully researched, practiced, and implemented.

3. If you secured an informational interview, it is your responsibility to begin the conversation with a topic "to pick Fred's brain." It was noted that the Hunt would not

deal with the question, "What do I want to do?" But obviously, at this point of the networking process, you must start with *something*, even if your direction is misguided. The more focused your direction, the better the quality of the ensuing referrals.

4. Once the conversation is engaged into substantive matters, you will be better served if Fred does the majority of the talking. The truly successful salesperson is a better listener than talker. You already know what is in your mind—the purpose of the visit is to learn Fred's mind. The first meeting is the appetizer, not the main course.

5. It is imperative to honor the time commitment (if any) that was made in securing the appointment. *("I won't take more than 20 minutes of your time.")* When the time expires, you should take control to offer an end to the conversation. Often, Fred will elect to continue on, but he must make that decision. Long sales calls are not always the best. It only gives the presenter a longer time to make a fatal error. Remember, most decisions are made in the first 4-5 minutes anyway.

. . . The truly successful salesperson is a better listener than talker.

The end of each visit should be closed with perhaps the most important comment/question uttered in the entire process:

> ALFRED: Fred, I really appreciate your thoughts on **(whatever he discussed)**. If you were in my shoes and were to pursue **(whatever he discussed)**, what two people would you contact?

If Fred has suggested a path that the careerist really does not wish to pursue, this is the time to re-direct the process. After receiving <u>one</u> name in keeping with Fred's line of thinking, Alfred T. might ask for advice in a specific career field more to his liking or direction. Obviously, with greater focus, the resulting referrals are of higher quality.

Fred's response might also be something like "*If I come up with any referrals, I'll let you know.*" He has just opened the door for your permission to initiate another call; your response would be:

> ALFRED: Boy, I really appreciate that. If I haven't heard from you in a couple of days, I'll give you a buzz so I can follow your lead.

Your network is built like a pyramid. If you have 15 visits out of the 25 letters you have written, then the object is to get 30 new names to perpetuate your campaign. Out of these 30 names, you will start the process all over—and secure 20 new appointments. From those 20 appointments, another 40 must be referred to you—which, of course, leads to 25 appointments—and so on.

I once had a careerist say, "*This sounds like Amway to me.*" He got it. No better assessment could be made. Self-marketing is multi-level marketing, and it is the lifeline of a successful careerist. If you fail to ask for the referral, your network will soon evaporate. By asking for the referral, your network never ends.

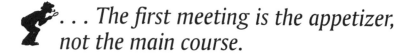

. . . The first meeting is the appetizer, not the main course.

Finally, each appointment should end with the comment:

> ALFRED: *Fred, I'd like to stay in touch with you. If it's OK, I'll initiate a follow-up phone call in about 45 days.*

Fred, not wishing to be offensive, will generally respond to the affirmative—all along, thinking that a follow-up will not occur. Fred has just never met a motivated Hunter for very lush Green Octobers.

The Self-Marketing Campaign
REPETITION, REPETITION, REPETITION
DRIP, DRIP, DRIP

Almost every large city in the United States has a Jim McIngvale—a person who dominates the local advertising marketplace. In Houston, "Mattress Mac" has become an institution with his loud, somewhat obtrusive, and simplistic commercials that unmercifully hawk the products of his store, Gallery Furniture.

If you turn on your car radio or surf the TV channels, his omnipresent face or distinctive voice can be seen or heard. His message is boringly clear—"No Back, Back, Back Orders"—"Immediate Delivery"—"Solid Wood Furniture." But the Granddaddy of all his promises consistently comes at the end of the commercial—"*Gallery Furniture Saves You Money!*" Mac then lifts a handful of greenbacks and shakes them at the camera. Outside of George Bush (Sr.), he is by far the most recognizable Houstonian—more so than the Mayor or any other civic, business, or spiritual leader.

How does this relate to Green Octobers? In the early 90's, I was fortunate to attend a communications seminar. The speaker (Lynn Sellers) coached all participants' methods to reinforce the most important selling features of their service offering. The seminar was held at a time when the movie, *The Firm*, adapted from the book written by John Grisham, was the hot release from Hollywood.

Lynn asked the audience:

> *"How many people here have seen the movie **The Firm?**"* Almost every hand in the audience went up. *"How many people can tell me the name of the lead character that was played by Tom Cruise?"* The blank looks on everyone's face provided no answer. *"How many people can tell me the name of the law firm? After all, that is the name of the movie."* Once again, the blank stares were all too painful.

At that point, Lynn redirected the question.

> *"Well, let me head somewhere else—I'm going to mention a slogan that I have recently heard, and I'm curious to see if anyone comes to mind. The slogan is "We will save you MONEY."*

Instantly, smirks were visible on all the faces, as the knowing nods acknowledged Mattress Mac without the mention of Gallery Furniture. But, Lynn kept probing.

> *"Let me ask a question to the ladies in the audience. Ladies, if you had your choice of dinner with Tom Cruise or Mattress Mac, who would you choose?"*

I'll give you two guesses to determine the leading vote getter. She continued:

> *"Now isn't that interesting, ladies. You seem to have this greater interest in Tom Cruise, but you can't remember the name of his character or the name of the firm for which he worked. But with the simple mention of a mere slogan, you can call to mind Mattress Mac. WHY? "*

The answer was very simple: **Repetition. Repetition. Repetition.**

Studies conducted by market researchers indicate that most consumers must hear the name of the product seven times before the listener will remember the name of the product, and that does not include remembering the most important selling features. Advertising executives continually remind clients that the key to advertising is to send a clear and consistent message; and if only a few ads are run, then the marketer has wasted money. It is the frequency and clarity of the message that forces the public to recall the product. All too often, a person will describe a humorous or creative ad; but then when asked which product was advertised, the same blank stare is reflected.

Is a careerist a product? Absolutely.

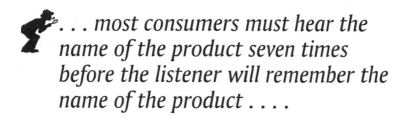

> *. . . most consumers must hear the name of the product seven times before the listener will remember the name of the product . . . .*

If these truisms work in marketing furniture, soap, or cars, then do the same principles apply in a job search campaign? You can bet on it.

The titans of business meet with lots of people and read more than one resumé. The bigger questions are: Which candidate will be remembered? Which resumé will make it to the top of the stack?

Up to this point in the process, Alfred T. Applicant has sent a transmittal letter and resumé, engaged in a brief phone conversation, and enjoyed one face-to-face visit with Friendly Fred. If the campaign ends here, then the advertising energies have, in all likelihood, been wasted.

> *. . . Is a careerist a product? Absolutely.*

The critical technique in finding the right job fit is the artful exercise of Chinese torture: *Drip. Drip. Drip.*

Alfred T. has expended huge efforts to get out a mailing and secure an appointment, but he has only planted the seed. It is now time to dig the irrigation ditch. The real trick in follow-up, however, is mastering the art of persistence (which is recognized as a good quality) without being a pest (which no one likes). The timing of the follow-up is also critical. Much like irrigation, if all the rain comes in one flood, the run-off is rapid and the damage is immense.

. . . The real trick in follow-up, however, is mastering the art of persistence . . . without being a pest . . . .

The most efficient and least invasive method to maintain a "state-of-mind awareness" with Friendly Fred is through multiple written communications. Once again, each word can be planned and tailored—and best of all, Alfred T. maintains a positive attitude because rejection becomes invisible to him.

The mailings (which will be described in subsequent chapters) may sit on Fred's desk for more than one day, thus providing Alfred T. an extra drip or two. And it is probably wise to include another copy of the resumé with <u>some</u> of the mailings because chances are that Fred has either forgotten Alfred T.'s sterling skill sets, has taken liberty of "retaining the resumé in the *active* files," or, in the worst case, discarded the resumé in File 13.

Most careerists probably regard the activities of securing appointments described in the previous chapter as the most important aspect of the job search. While such activities are undoubtedly the most *difficult* part of the process and receive the greatest level of rejection, they are <u>not</u> the most important aspect.

It should be remembered that sales professionals seldom close the deal on the first call. Jobs don't exist; they emerge. Seeds planted in the ground don't bloom unless watered.

The most important aspect of Alfred T.'s job search is the follow-up activity. The processes (described in the ensuing chapters) are generally overlooked and yet, are the easiest to accomplish.

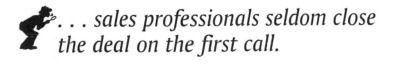

. . . sales professionals seldom close the deal on the first call.

Paul Harvey was fond of saying, "Page two . . . the rest of the story." Therefore, the "rest of the <u>self-marketing</u> story" will focus on **repetition, repetition, repetition—drip, drip, drip.**

. . . Seeds planted in the ground don't bloom unless watered.

There are many furniture stores in Houston, but the most furniture is sold at the store owned by Mattress Mac. Have Houstonians purchased the best furniture available? Did Tenneco hire the best Policy and Procedure Writer? The successful careerist now needs to practice the art of follow-up, always being persistent without being a pest.

THE THANK YOU LETTER

In the last 25 years, the business community has been represented poorly by the appalling lack of written communications skills of many of the business leaders and participants. Obviously, this blight resulted from a breakdown in our educational system—but its effects have been masked by the wonders of technology.

To some extent, the sore has been covered by a 21st century bandage. Spell check replaced spelling bees; e-mails replaced position papers and executive summaries. As <u>sciences</u> and math were emphasized (which effectively propelled the computer generation), the <u>art</u> of language acuity and fluidity was relegated to second place.

Many of the techniques that Alfred T. has executed up to this point are processes requiring implementation. Processes take a scientific form; there are standards and some level of predictability. The manner in which his campaign moves forward needs to take an artistic form. Creativity, flair, timing, and spontaneity will move his resumé from Friendly Fred's desk drawer to the Employment Office.

Writing a thank you letter to Fred not only makes good business for Alfred T., it is also good manners. The natural tendency is to rush home after the interview, prepare the correspondence, and immediately put it in the mailbox. That's what Miss Manners would do.

A bit of strategy at this point can pay big dividends and set the pace for subsequent steps. If the visit with Fred was on Monday, he will likely maintain some mental awareness of Alfred T. for a few days. It should be remembered that marketers are trying to maintain "state-of-the-mind awareness." The problem begins to surface about Thursday or Friday because Alfred T. is now out of sight and out of mind.

Often, when watching late night television, I have viewed the *same commercial* multiple times within a short time span. I was turned off. The advertiser wasted money on a per insertion basis and, at the same time, alienated me. The same is true in self-marketing. The ideal time for the thank you note to arrive at Fred's office is a week following the interview—when Alfred T. is fading from memory and not the next day when the memory is still fresh.

The style and flair of the note is very important. The stationery size that differs from the norm provides a means of calling special attention. Another effective medium is a heavy-stock note card with a monogrammed or embossed look. Assuming Alfred T. has pleasing penmanship (another lost art!), a handwritten presentation stands out from the stack of business correspondence. A good fountain pen is a worthwhile investment; the drama that unfolds will certainly outshine the Walgreen's offering of a Bic roller ball.

> *... The ideal time for the thank you note to arrive at Fred's office is a week following the interview ....*

Once again, our old friends, Short and To The Point, will serve Alfred T. well.

> Dear Fred,
>
> Thanks for the time you invested in meeting with me last week. Your thoughts on **(whatever he talked about)** were very enlightening and appreciated. I will be contacting Bill Bright and Sam Smith **(Fred's two referrals)** immediately. I look forward to our next conversation and visit.
>
> Warm regards,
>
> *Alfred T. Applicant*
>
> Alfred T. Applicant

Does this imply that e-mail is not an effective form of communication? No, technology is definitely a desired medium of the business world and provides instant benefits. However, the problem with e-mail is that it is hard to touch and feel; and if the message is printed, Alfred T.'s presentation will look like everyone else's. The delete button can be pushed very quickly with e-mail, and the correspondence does not sit on the desktop very long.

E-mail is an effective medium when time is of the essence, but pen and paper have a greater opportunity to make a marketing statement.

The timing and flair of the thank you note are of much greater importance than the actual words. It needs to feel good, seem classy, and create a buzz. A restatement of qualifications is definitely not in order during this communication. This note is an attempt to begin a bonding process, one that places a "personhood" to the resumé and Fred's memory of Alfred T.'s interview.

... E-mail is an effective medium when time is of the essence, but pen and paper have a greater opportunity to make a marketing statement.

The idea of sending a thank you letter after an interview process is certainly not revolutionary. It is a natural tendency to write the note if Alfred T. requested the appointment; but, shockingly, it is not often written when the candidate was recruited by a headhunter or by Fred. Both circumstances deserve good manners and thus, a marketing opportunity is not lost.

Good manners have no boundaries and are seldom over exercised. The thank you note is a marketing opportunity to "*make you money*" and is the first **DRIP** in the irrigation canal.

It's a time when the Liberal Arts students can finally revel in their education.

---

*. . . Writing a thank you letter . . .
not only makes good business . . .
it is also good manners.*

The Self-Marketing Campaign
"CARBON" COPIES (CC:)

In a previous chapter, Alfred T. expended extraordinary efforts to secure an appointment, and chances are good that Friendly Fred was not hiring and never will. At first blush, it seems like an incredible waste of time.

But the most important words uttered during that visit occurred when Alfred T. said:

> *"Fred, I really appreciate your thoughts on* (**whatever he discussed**). *If you were in my shoes and were to pursue* (**whatever he discussed**), *what two people would you contact?"*

By asking for the referrals, Alfred T.'s network never ends. The stage has been set for a new appointment call. You may recall that when Alfred T. wrote Fred, his transmittal letter stated:

> *"Of particular note, I am skilled in organizational development processes dealing with human capital integration that is necessary in business mergers and acquisitions."*

But suppose that during the visit, Fred steered the conversation in a different direction. Perhaps Fred was aware of opportunities in sales training and curriculum development, and being aware of Alfred T.'s multiple skill sets, he provided the names of Bill Bright and Sam Smith as potential contacts.

In contacting Fred's referrals, Alfred T. can repeat his letter writing process, but he tailors the letter to meet the changing circumstances. However, the most important aspect of <u>this</u> transmittal is the notation "CC: Friendly Fred" at the end of the letter.

Dear Bill,

Friendly Fred suggested that I contact you.

Enclosed is my biographical summary reflecting 23 years experience in human resources management in both the corporate sector and the staffing industry. Of particular note, I am skilled in sales training and program development. This aspect of my career has produced my best work and greatest professional joys.

I'll contact you next week to request a time when we might visit.

Warm regards,

Alfred T. Applicant

Alfred T. Applicant

CC: Friendly Fred

The cc: notation serves dual purposes. First, it leads Mr. Bill Bright to the assumption that Alfred T. and Friendly Fred are best buddies. But perhaps more importantly, it provides another opportunity for Alfred T. to *DRIP* on Friendly Fred. The letter written to Bill Bright can be sent immediately upon receiving the referral.

However, the timing of the copy mailed to Fred is critical. The thank you note hit Fred's desk seven days after the original appointment. The copy of the letter sent to Bill Bright needs to be received by Fred in fourteen days. *DRIP.*

Of course, Alfred T. received two referrals, not just one. Being the enterprising careerist, he will also write Sam Smith immediately upon receiving the referral and naturally, send a carbon copy to Friendly Fred. The date that this copy is received by Fred will also be controlled by Alfred; it will hit Fred's desk twenty-one days after the original appointment. *DRIP.*

The irrigation canal is beginning to widen.

. . . In contacting Fred's referrals, Alfred T. can repeat his letter writing process, but he tailors the letter to meet the changing circumstances.

It has now been three weeks since Alfred T. met with Friendly Fred, and the meeting has been reinforced with three pieces of correspondence. In the mailing that went to Fred in the second week, Alfred needs to enclose another copy of his resumé. It is quite likely that Fred has forgotten Alfred's skill sets, misfiled the resumé, or perhaps discarded it completely.

The "rest of the story" continues.

 . . . the timing of the copy is critical.

The Self-Marketing Campaign
CLIPPINGS, REFERENCE LETTERS, AND PHONE CALLS

A pattern is beginning to emerge. It is now dawning on Friendly Fred that Alfred T. is not going to disappear into the woodwork. Just as the memory is about to fade away, here comes another mailing. However, the beauty of orchestrating a follow-up campaign with written correspondence is that actions imply persistence, but they are not perceived as "in your face."

Several other *DRIP* opportunities remain at Alfred T.'s disposal: clippings, reference letters, and phone calls.

A successful careerist needs to become a consistent reader of business articles. Since Friendly Fred works at General Motors, Alfred T. must make it a goal to find some mention of GM in the newspaper or other publication. The nature of the clipping is of no importance. The story might be an announcement of GM's new model line or a brief mention as innocuous as the declaration of a quarterly stock dividend. Furthermore, the mention does not necessarily need to have pertinence to Alfred T.'s discussion with Fred.

The clipping might not even refer to General Motors, but it could be an article that would appeal to Fred's interests. But by mailing <u>any</u> clipping to Fred, Alfred T. is extending his visible dialogue and maintaining "state-of-the-mind awareness."

Accompanying the clipping, a short note (either handwritten or in traditional business correspondence) should say:

> *"Fred, saw this nice mention of your company in the Journal. Congratulations. Free publicity is always the best kind!"*

Once again, the timing of the mailing becomes a strategic decision. Four weeks after the initial visit, the mailman needs to deliver his continual care package to Fred. *DRIP.*

The irrigation canal is beginning to conduct a steady trickle.

 . . . A successful careerist needs to become a consistent reader of business articles.

A simple roster of Alfred T.'s references (with contact numbers listed) provides yet another *DRIP* opportunity. Accompanying the mailing, Alfred will likely include a short note and the third copy of his resumé—just in case Fred can't put his hands on either of the first two. This does not imply that Fred requested this information, but Alfred is just looking for another chance to utilize the services of the Pony Express. By now, you can probably guess when the delivery will arrive: Week Five. *DRIP.*

. . . the timing of the mailing becomes a strategic decision.

After all of this correspondence, Week Six seems to be the right time for Alfred T. to return to hand-to-hand combat. It is finally time to pick up the phone and initiate a call to Friendly Fred. At the end his original appointment, the comment was made:

```
Fred, I'd like to stay in touch with you. If
it's OK, I'll initiate a follow-up call in
about 45 days.
```

At the time, Fred was unsuspecting. Hopefully, this call will pass through Sally Sue with ease. (She certainly recognizes the name by now!) Our good friends, Short and To The Point, return as the preferred telephone style.

```
Hi, Fred, this is Alfred T. When we visited on
(date of the appointment), you suggested that I
should call you back in about 45 days. Have
there been any new developments at General
Motors?
```

The conversation may take multiple directions, but the *DRIP* cycle has now been completed. Alfred T. can use this opportunity to report on his conversations with Bill Bright and/ or Sam Smith. It is another opportunity to ask for other referrals or suggestions. Naturally, the conversation should close with Alfred's statement:

```
I'll continue to stay in touch. If the right
opportunity surfaces at General Motors that
would utilize my skill sets, I hope you will
give me a call.
```

Mattress Mac would be proud of Alfred T. The message was consistent and clear, and he was disciplined to ask for the order.

 . . . the beauty of orchestrating a follow-up campaign with written correspondence is . . . not perceived as "in your face."

PART III

GREEN OCTOBERS

LIFETIME SELF-MARKETING

In the first chapter, it was noted that the pursuit for Green Octobers was a *continual* activity—a lifetime habit. The preceding chapters have outlined activities of a job seeker, but not necessarily the committed careerist.

What is the difference between the two? Are the behaviors really that different between an unemployed person seeking work and the employed person wishing to change his/her career path? Not if one adopts the premise of lifetime self-marketing.

When I left the *perceived* security of the corporate world in 1980, a colleague warned me of the perils of my newly chosen profession as an executive search consultant. *"Wow,"* he said, *"that job requires a lot of self-promotion."* The comment made me pause.

In my mind, change was occurring because I was bored with the support role of corporate Human Resources. In retrospect, my friend's comment was very accurate; however, experience has taught me that self-promotion is a necessity of <u>every</u> *committed* careerist, whether in corporate life or self-employment.

Self-promotion may sound vain and egocentric, but it is absolutely essential to ensure October to be always Green. The opportunity to maintain contact with all the Friendly Freds of the world is limitless.

I had the pleasure of watching a sky-rocketing career of a young man who was a peer of my three grown sons. He had incredible work habits and an innate business sense. While in college, he frequently forwarded articles to me that pertained to the staffing industry. I also received an annual Christmas greeting and birthday card from this rising entrepreneur. It was no surprise that he later founded a company that was recognized as the fastest growing, privately held firm in Houston—and his company achieved this astounding recognition when he was age 29. Drip, Drip, Drip.

Successful politicians have also learned the value of the Drip Theory. In the mid-80's, I was invited to a function where Jack Kemp was the featured speaker, and personally visited with him for all of about two minutes. It is easier than you might think to obtain rosters of attendees at large-scale gatherings. Imagine my shock when I received a package from him six weeks later with a copy of a book he authored—personally signed, of course. I remained on his Christmas card list until he ran for Vice President of the United States. Guess who I voted for?

How many training courses have you attended where there was a participant's listing? How many church or neighborhood directories have cluttered your desk drawers? What are the special interest groups where you were an active participant? Every step of our life, we connect to people, but discipline is required to stay in touch with them. Birthday cards and

Christmas greetings are obvious and easy connections, but the "reach out and touch someone" method of just saying "hi" on a frequent basis creates a far more favorable impression.

. . . Self-promotion may sound vain and egocentric, but it is absolutely essential to ensure October to be always Green.

Computerization is a wonderful tool to organize and calendar the information required to effectively fertilize the Green grass of October. The tendency is to be very selective and focused in maintaining a small network of recent contacts. Just the opposite is true. My *"Golden Rules"* mailing list is quite lengthy and provides a forum to place my name in front of multiple decision makers on a monthly and/or quarterly basis.

. . . Every step of our life, we connect to people, but discipline is required to stay in touch with them.

Each year, I review where new business opportunities originated, and marvel how seemingly insignificant some contacts were at the time of the initial meeting. However, routine follow-up produced a meaningful relationship, both in business and personally. Sales-minded careerists never know where the next order will originate, but they do know that nothing will originate until relationships are watered. Proper irrigation requires diligent work in ditch digging.

 . . . Sales-minded careerists never know where the next order will originate, but they do know that nothing will originate until relationships are watered.

Generally women understand, to a greater degree than men, that one is "always on stage" in life. My wife will not make a simple trip to the grocery store unless she is dressed and groomed in a manner that appropriately presents her to the world. *("You never know who you might run into.")* The same is true in networking; we are never given a second chance to make a first impression.

Lifetime self-marketing is facilitated if Alfred T. is genuine in his quest to become a "people person." However, the thought that certain people are "natural born salesmen" is really just a myth. I have never seen a baby emerge from the womb to hear someone remark, *"He looks like a seven-pound, six-ounce closer."* The committed careerist must be aware of surroundings, organized and disciplined in contact and follow-up, and sincere and genuine in building a relationship.

Self-promotion suddenly seems to be a *good* thing, not vain and egocentric. Alfred T. learned that cold calls received frozen receptions. Likewise, it is no accident that a committed careerist "seems to know everyone," effectively communicates with those resources, and thus, gains personal advancement.

When these behaviors become part of daily life, one becomes a *pro-active* committed careerist, instead of a *reactive* job seeker.

---

 *. . . I have never seen . . .
a seven-pound, six-ounce closer.*

THE RESUMÉ

All books written on the job search process devote some attention to the preparation of a resumé. As mentioned earlier, there are many <u>entire</u> books focusing on this singular topic. However, since the central theme of the Hunt is *self*-marketing techniques, all thoughts on resumé preparation offered here will be conceptual in nature and will support the central theme.

My lack of emphasis on resumé writing underscores a belief on how the careerist is to spend his/her time. To be sure, the resumé is an integral tool. But when things move too slowly to satisfy the job seeker, the natural tendency is to revert back to tweak the resumé, often with the false perception that the resumé is the problem, not activities required in self-marketing.

Many people are willing to spend significant efforts on this document because the result is within their control. Conversely, self-marketing requires cooperation of outsiders—a far more difficult constituency. Thus, endless hours are often spent massaging the work for just the right effect. One would think that the Magna Carta was being written.

The real truth is that a resumé is an advertisement for the careerist, and the document has only one major purpose—to help secure an appointment. Any good ad is crafted to support and drive sales efforts. Such is true with the resumé exercise.

> *. . . when things move too slowly to satisfy the job seeker, the natural tendency is to revert back to tweak the resumé, often with the false perception that the resumé is the problem, not activities required in self-marketing.*

- The resumé provides a sense of organization to one's career. It is a time to memorize the dates of employment, the sequence of experiences, and the accomplishments during each job. I am always baffled when a person can't recall the date of a career event or the name of a supervisor or executive team member. It is a clue that the person is seeking a new job for a reason—perhaps he/she wasn't paying attention while at work!

- The resumé is an opportunity for a person to exhibit a sense of uniqueness—to communicate an individual sense of personhood. Something needs to jump out to the reader that separates the resumé from the rejection stack. However, there is a very fine line that must be walked in this consideration. It is important that the uniqueness is subtle and does not vary totally from the mainstream. The result must always be professional, not "artsy" or overdramatic.

Nonetheless, a certain sense of uniqueness in the resumé can create a small advantage to the careerist.

- The resumé provides a forum to amplify strengths and accomplishments. The most powerful statement to accomplish this purpose is to highlight *results*. Conversely, it should also be crafted to minimize one's shortcomings.

- Resumés can be (and should be) tailored to meet differing needs. When the careerist has prior knowledge of a particular job requirement, it is appropriate to re-position his/her skill sets to best address the need.

There are several characteristics that should be incorporated into every resumé:

- The length of the document should **never** exceed two pages. Most resumés are scanned, not read. Remember, this is an advertisement, not a job description.

- The "best stuff" in one's career should be recorded "up front"—i.e., in the top half of the first page. An obvious problem might result if one's "best stuff" occurred three employers ago—and if the resumé is written in a chronological order. (*Ways to avoid this will follow!*)

- The appearance of the document is of equal importance to its contents. Like most ads, there must be ample "white space." The weight of the paper should be at least 20 pound, and the color is generally limited to white, beige or gray. The usage of varying font sizes, CAPITAL LETTERS, **bold print**, <u>underscoring</u>, and *italics* add interest—but should be applied ***<u>consistently</u>***. For example, all job titles underscored, all company names in all caps and bold, etc.

- Leave room for intrigue. Comprehensive descriptions are not helpful. The document should promote interest for the reader and leave room for conversation in the interview. Complete sentences are seldom utilized in resumé writing and actions verbs are needed to add impact.

- The contact information at the top of the resumé should reflect only the number of a cell phone that the job seeker has in his/her possession at all times. In this manner, response time is immediate and personal.

. . . Most resumés are scanned, not read. Remember: this is an advertisement, not a job description.

The <u>functional</u> resumé focuses on skill sets and accomplishments (typically noted on page one), thus minimizing the chronology of dates/employers on page two. There are some obvious advantages in this presentation.

- If we are intent on reporting our "best stuff" up front, yet our most sterling accomplishments occurred ten years ago, the functional resumé allows a more flexible format—one not tied to time.

- If a person is anxious to make an extreme career shift—i.e., pursue a job interest that is not necessarily supported by previous work experiences—the functional resumé allows the writer to present skill sets to support the goal, rather than work histories.

- Since the functional resumé minimizes work history, this format is an obvious advantage to someone who has been a bit of a job hopper or who has encountered frequent stretches of unemployment.

The chronological resumé is more frequently utilized. Many readers develop a distrust (as if something is being hidden) if the current employer (and subsequent history) are not reflected "up front" in plain view. Obviously, this format forces the writer to place all accomplishments at the time they occurred, which might not be the most advantageous placement.

Frequently, a person will have progressed through several differing jobs while remaining in the employ of the same company. The entirety of the employment dates should remain on the line reflecting the company name, and the dates of specific jobs should be imbedded into the description of those jobs.

Additionally, many people "change" companies simply by corporate acquisition/merger, thus resulting in a name change of the employer. In such cases, it is preferable to reflect the entirety of the tenure by noting the current employer *and predecessor or subsidiary companies* in the major listing (and total date history), then follow with subparagraphs to denote differing ownerships. This method minimizes the appearance of "job hopping."

. . . The contact information . . . should reflect only the number of a cell phone . . . . In this manner, response time is immediate and personal.

Generally, the best presentation is to design a <u>combination</u> resumé. This type of presentation begins with a brief Summary section (not an Objective) that provides a 4-5 sentence overview as to who you are, followed by an indented, bulleted listing of 3-4 of your most outstanding accomplishments or skill sets. These two sections should adorn the top half of page one, with the chronological listing of employers (and accompanying descriptions) beginning mid-way on the first page. This combination provides necessary flexibility inherent in the functional resumé, yet provides the reader comfort of the more traditionally chronological presentation.

The resumé is a critical marketing tool, but it is not a time-consuming activity. The essence of the Summary statement is *"This is what you are getting ready to read."* The Accomplishments need to be brief, specific, and quantifiable. The Work History and Education categories record the facts and add meat to these first two sections. The style and appearance is critical—much like "Dress for Success."

The resumé never gets the careerist the job; it only opens the door for the Hunt to begin.

. . . Any good ad is crafted to support and drive sales efforts. Such is true with the resumé exercise.

GOING TO THE DRIVING RANGE

A number of years ago, I frequently presented seminars on job search techniques to people who had been negatively affected by corporate downsizing. Often, at the beginning of the presentation, I took a $100 bill and made a bold offer:

> *"I'm offering a learning challenge as we explore new career opportunities together. If, after the end of this seminar, you implement **all of the techniques** that we discuss and then don't find the job of your choice in 90 days, this $100 belongs to you."*

No one ever claimed the $100.

It was a safe bet. Very few people attack the problem with the intensity, level of commitment, and awareness of detail to implement *all of the techniques*. The goal of this book was to unveil self-marketing options and stimulate thinking.

One participant whined that *all of the techniques* encompassed a lot of work! Since he was unemployed, I bluntly asked him, *"What else are you doing with your time?"*

I'll never forget the comment of one participant who had completed the workshop and said, *"No wonder you made the offer. Doing all of this is a full-time job."* For the unemployed, she was right.

It is often said, *"It's easier to find a job if you already have a job."* However, the networking that results in "face time" with Friendly Fred normally requires time during working hours—a luxury not always afforded to the employed worker.

The unemployed job seeker serious about the Hunt must be disciplined about all the normal, daily routines. The alarm needs to be set at the time that one would arise to prepare for work. The most successful careerist prepares by dressing in normal business attire, recognizing that he/she is always on stage to the world.

. . . Very few people attack the problem with the intensity, level of commitment, and awareness of detail to implement all of the techniques.

It is also helpful to have a friend who will make a spare office available so that the daily environment is in the workplace. Thus, phone calls can be received professionally, and messages will not be bungled by eight-year-old Johnny at home. If an office outside the home is not a viable option, it is imperative that the job seeker provides a cell phone number (rather than a home number) for all return calls. Greater control is gained as to who answers the phone.

All sales professionals are accustomed to accountability for a quota of the number of sales calls made. The <u>successful</u> professionals exceed the minimum numbers, realizing the greater number of opportunities, more sales will follow. Such is true in networking for the job searcher. It is a numbers game, but one measured by disciplined efforts.

When I started my first business in 1980, there were no clients; thus, I was unemployed. My "job" was to have four appointments per day—8:30, 10:30, 1:30, and 3:30. It is easy to understand my times for the appointments, since I had no money to buy breakfasts, luncheons, or drinks.

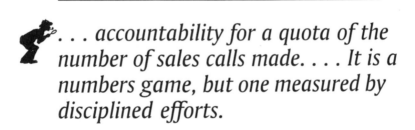

. . . accountability for a quota of the number of sales calls made. . . . It is a numbers game, but one measured by disciplined efforts.

It is relatively easy to meet your quota for one day, but the trick is the internal commitment to a **daily quota**. Let's assume that Alfred T. establishes his quota as two per day—one appointment in the morning, the other in the afternoon. Since there are 21 workdays in a normal month, he will complete 42 appointment calls in the first month.

Of course, he must also write 42 thank you letters, mail new letters to 84 referrals (with "carbon" copies sent), find 42 clippings, and so on. By the time he has implemented the **daily plan** for 2-3 months, he has already visited with 80-120 Friendly Fred's and follow-up each with five additional mailings. The key is reaching the goal every day, and not sporadically.

. . . It is relatively easy to meet your quota for one day, but the trick is the internal commitment to a daily quota.

It is also a natural tendency to become excited when the first "serious" possibility surfaces. Often the networker forgets to implement the daily plan and diverts focus to this single new opportunity. Such a person will encounter frequent disappointment and will be relegated to accepting the first job offered, rather than the best job available. The disciplined careerist will continue the process in a multi-tasking manner so that several options may be considered.

It is worth repeating again: the Hunt requires discipline and hard work. Everyone wants to shoot 72 on the golf course, but the long hours on the driving range don't hold as much appeal.

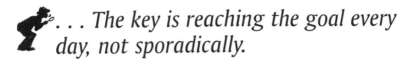

. . . The key is reaching the goal every day, not sporadically.

As mentioned earlier, a huge obstacle to the self-marketing process is overcoming ego issues, especially the disappointment of a (seemingly) failed experience. He/she often wants to keep the matter private which, of course, serves as a detriment. Since it is more "acceptable" in the 21st Century to be in job transition, the most successful careerist will feel free "to come out of the closet" quickly.

Jobs don't exist; they emerge! It requires effort to uncover that opportunity, and opportunity will not knock unless Alfred T. asks for it.

Real progress in the Hunt for Green Octobers only occurs when the careerist commits to a specific number of appointments per day, which translates to a weekly quota, and eventually, a monthly achievement. If Alfred T. sent his original 25 letters and achieved 15 appointments, he then obtained 30 referrals. These 30 produced 20 appointments, which yielded 40 referrals.

By now, the picture is pretty clear: **It's a numbers game.**

All successful sales professionals commit to a high activity process. The big hurdle is to convince careerists that they are **in the sales business, too.**

Once a person has encountered 60-85 appointment calls, i.e., "face time"—whether the call is "informational" or a specific job interview—**only then** has Alfred T. *really* conducted a job search.

It would be nice if the trumpets would blow and everyone would bow at Alfred T.'s knee. But it's not going to happen!

Someone else is mounting a more effective sales campaign, and thus, the best Policy and Procedure Writer will go unhired.

It is interesting to note that each singular step of the process is relatively easy to achieve; collectively, however, it might seem a daunting task.

With work, Alfred T. *can* write down 250 names of people he knows. He *can* then pick the "best 25." With grit in his teeth, he *can* make the calls to secure "X" number of appointments. It is not too hard to ask for two referrals. Then the process repeats itself, but all along, keeping the eye on Fred. A thank you letter, copies to the two referrals, a clipping and a reference listing, finally a phone call—it accumulates to a **HUGE DRIP.**

All of these things, *Alfred can do.*

> *. . . Once a person has encountered 60-85 appointment calls . . . only then has Alfred T. really conducted a job search.*

The greatest hurdle to accomplishment is to overcome the rejection. It is important to break the tasks down to small, measurable steps, then take delight in the joy of achieving the daily goal.

The Hunt is over.

The caller on the other end of the telephone is Friendly Fred from General Motors; he is extending a job offer to Alfred T. as a *Senior* Policy and Procedure Writer. Alfred can savor the moment because he spent the appropriate time at the driving range.

Realizing that his dream job did not exist, but needed to emerge, he *artfully and repetitively* applied the Chinese torture: Drip. Drip. Drip.

In almost every case, there is an opportunity to negotiate the offer to maximize Alfred's position. Even if the offer is acceptable immediately, it would be wise *"to sleep on it overnight"* and then call Fred back with a modification to some term that represents an enhancement. Every employer always leaves "a little meat on the bone"; by re-positioning the offer (even if ever so slightly), Alfred will set the stage for greater respect in his future employment. The dilemma, of course, is not to push the limit to an extreme whereby an adverse relationship is created.

Alfred's headhunter friend still has lots of business, but he quickly saw the difference in taking matters into his own hands.

Now is the time for Alfred to go to the golf course and revel in the joys of the Green October.

SUMMARY OF THE
SELF-MARKETING PROCESS

1. Identify 250 contacts.

2. Select 25 as the most influential.

3. Write 25 letters requesting an appointment.

4. Follow-up calls to obtain appointments. Set goal of at least 15 appointments.

5. Get 30 referrals from the 15 people that you visit. Set goal of meeting at least 18 of these new referrals.

6. Write a thank you letter to the original 15.

7. Send a copy (cc:) of the letter requesting an appointment (of the "new 30") back to the person who referred you.

8. Send a listing of references to anyone you have visited.

9. Send clippings/news articles regarding one of your prospect's company with a note acknowledging your awareness.

10. Make 45-day follow-up call.

The process repeats itself—more thank you notes, "carbon" copies, references, and clippings to new referrals.

Drip. Drip. Drip.